My CELLO Practice Journal

This journal belongs to:

_____

_____

Copyright © 2020 EDventure Learning LLC

All rights reserved. This book or any portion thereof may not be reproduced or used in any manner whatsoever without the express written permission of the publisher.

Image credits: Freepik (cover, pp. 2-3, 7, 47, 71, 166); NingZk V.|Rawpixel (p. 2); bimbimkha|Freepik (pp. 2-3); OpenClipart-Vectors|Pixabay (pp. 3, 71); Lisitsaimage|Dreamstime (p. 23); Rawpixel (p. 95); pch.vector|Freepik (p. 119); Seijirooooooooooo|Dreamstime (p. 143)

Printed in the United States of America
ISBN: 978-1-64824-010-2

EDventure Learning LLC
5601 State Route 31 #1296
Clay, NY 13039

www.edventurelearning.com

Email us at hello@edventurelearning.com

Table of Contents

How to Use This Book	1
My Repertoire List	6
My Starting Point	8
The Year Ahead	9
Practice Log	11
The Year in Review	167
Reference	171
Cello Fingering Chart	173
Musical Glossary	174
Answer Key	176
Notes	180
Staff Paper	186

How to Use This Book

Hi! Thanks for picking up this journal! It's awesome that you're learning how to play the cello. Whether you're just starting out or have been playing for a few years already, this book is here to help you have a great year.

This journal is meant to help you make the most out of your practice time. We want to help you do your best and have fun as you get better and better at playing the cello. By filling out this journal, you can:

- learn to recognize what you're doing well and what to work on
- set goals for yourself
- keep track of what you practice
- share your progress with your teacher
- see how far you've come and feel great about what you've accomplished

Here's how to use each part of the journal to set yourself up for success:

Repertoire List

Use these pages to keep a list of all the songs you learn to play. Write down the title and composer of each piece, along with the date you added it to the list. Check the "M" box when you have the song memorized. Watch as your list grows, and be proud of yourself for all of the songs you've learned!

My Starting Point and The Year Ahead

These pages will help you think about how you're playing now and what you hope your playing will be like a year from now. Use it to set goals and what you will do to reach them. Your teacher can help you think about goals that might be a good fit for you right now. You can look back on your goals all year to help remind you of what you want to do and what you need to do to get there.

Practice Log

This is where you will spend the most time in the journal, keeping track of your lessons, daily practice, and monthly goals. The practice log is divided into four-week sections.

Each week, you will fill out a two-page spread. With your teacher, you'll fill out the Lesson Recap with what you worked on during your lesson. Your teacher will also help you fill out your Practice Plan with your assignments for the week. Fill out what you practiced each day during the week. At the end of the week, fill out the Weekly Recap and bring it to show your teacher at your next lesson.

Here is an example of how to use your weekly pages:

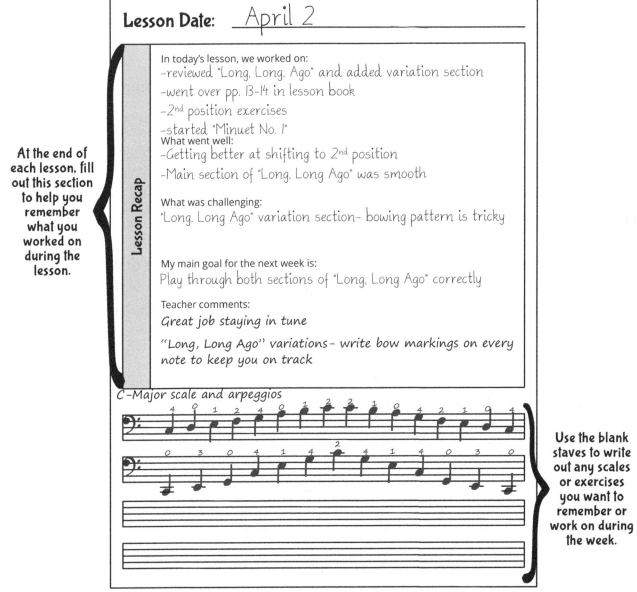

Set a goal for how much you will practice each week.

This week, I will practice __20__ minutes per day for __5__ days.

Before the end of your lesson, you and your teacher should fill out this part of the practice plan together. Fill out what you plan to practice (exercises, pieces, pages in your books, etc.) and what to focus on while playing (tempo, dynamics, certain measures, etc.).

Practice Plan

What to Practice:	What to Focus On:	Su M Tu W Th F Sa
C major scales and arpeggios (warm up)	Smooth bowing, steady beat, increase speed	♪ ♪ ♪ ♪ ♪ ♪ ♪
Lesson book p. 15	Work on shifting smoothly to 2nd position	♪ ♪ ♪ ♪ ♪ ♪ ♪
"Long, Long Ago"	Focus on bowing pattern in variation section	♪ ♪ ♪ ♪ ♪ ♪ ♪
"Minuet No. 1"	Follow the fingerings shown for 2nd position	♪ ♪ ♪ ♪ ♪ ♪ ♪
Complete Theory Book pp. 12-14		♩ ♩ ♩ ♩ ♩ ♩ ♩
		♩ ♩ ♩ ♩ ♩ ♩ ♩
		♩ ♩ ♩ ♩ ♩ ♩ ♩
		♩ ♩ ♩ ♩ ♩ ♩ ♩

For each day that you practice each of your assignments, color in a music note.

Practice Time (min)	Su	M	Tu	W	Th	F	Sa	Total
	20		25	20		20	15	100

Write down how many minutes you practice each day. At the end of the week, add up the total.

At the end of the week, before your next lesson, fill out this section. Think about what was great and what was hard this week. Write down anything you want to talk to your teacher about at your lesson.

Weekly Recap

What went well this week:
- Bowing is much better on "Long, Long Ago"
- Understood all the theory pages

What was challenging this week:
"Minuet No. 1"- keeping the tempo steady during position shifts

Questions/Comments:
Do we have a date/time yet for the spring recital?

Parent Signature: _Anne Higgins_

After every four weeks, you'll come to a "Monthly Check-In," shown on the right. This gives you a chance to think back over the past month. You can celebrate the things you did well and think about what challenges you faced. This will help you figure out what to work on the next month.

At the end of the month, you'll also find a "Just for Fun" page, with a puzzle, coloring page, or other activity to complete. Answer keys for the puzzles are found in the Reference section in the back of the book.

When a new month begins, you'll find "The Month Ahead." Here, you can write down your goals for the next four weeks. Think about techniques you want to get better at, new songs you want to learn, recitals or concerts you need to prepare for, and anything else you may want to work on for the month. Keep these goals in mind as you and your teacher select what to practice throughout the month.

Monthly Check-In

In the past month, I am proud that I...

In the past month, my biggest challenge was...

The Month Ahead

In the next month, I want to continue...

Next month, I want to get better at...

Next month, I want to learn...

Other notes:

The Year in Review

At the end of the 52 weeks, you'll find "The Year in Review," where you can celebrate the amazing year you've had. This will give you a chance to think about your wins and challenges for the whole year. Look back on everything you've learned and be proud of yourself! Then, gear up and dream big for the next year of your cello journey!

Reference

At the end of the book is all sorts of useful information to help you as you play this year. You'll find a fingering chart and a glossary of musical terms. This is also where you'll find the answers to the puzzles found throughout the book. In the very back, you'll find blank lined notepaper and staff paper. Use these however you want throughout the year.

We hope that at the end of the year, you find that practicing often and well has made you a stronger musician. We hope you are very proud of how hard you've worked and how far you've come. We also hope that this has been a fun year and that you're motivated to keep playing. If this journal has helped you this year, pick up another one and let us stay with you for another year of your musical journey.

Happy playing!

My Repertoire List
(Songs I Can Play)

Keep a list of the pieces you've learned. Check the "M" box when you have the song memorized.

#	Title	Composer	Date	M
1				
2				
3				
4				
5				
6				
7				
8				
9				
10				
11				
12				
13				
14				
15				

#	Title	Composer	Date	M
16				
17				
18				
19				
20				
21				
22				
23				
24				
25				
26				
27				
28				
29				
30				

My Starting Point

Right now, the things about playing the cello that I feel good about are...

Right now, the things about playing the cello that feel hard are...

The Year Ahead

This year, I want to get better at...

This year, I want to learn to play...

This year, I want to continue...

Other goals or notes:

The Month Ahead

In the next month, I want to continue…

In the next month, I want to get better at…

In the next month, I want to learn…

Other notes:

Lesson Date: _____

Lesson Recap

In today's lesson, we worked on:

What went well:

What was challenging:

My main goal for the next week is:

Teacher comments:

Practice Plan

This week, I will practice _____ minutes per day for _____ days.

What to Practice:	What to Focus On:	Su M Tu W Th F Sa
		♩ ♩ ♩ ♩ ♩ ♩ ♩
		♩ ♩ ♩ ♩ ♩ ♩ ♩
		♩ ♩ ♩ ♩ ♩ ♩ ♩
		♩ ♩ ♩ ♩ ♩ ♩ ♩
		♩ ♩ ♩ ♩ ♩ ♩ ♩
		♩ ♩ ♩ ♩ ♩ ♩ ♩
		♩ ♩ ♩ ♩ ♩ ♩ ♩
		♩ ♩ ♩ ♩ ♩ ♩ ♩

Practice Time (min)	Su	M	Tu	W	Th	F	Sa	Total

Weekly Recap

What went well this week:

What was challenging this week:

Questions/Comments:

Parent Signature: _____

Lesson Date: _____

Lesson Recap

In today's lesson, we worked on:

What went well:

What was challenging:

My main goal for the next week is:

Teacher comments:

Practice Plan

This week, I will practice _____ minutes per day for _____ days.

What to Practice:	What to Focus On:	Su	M	Tu	W	Th	F	Sa
		♩	♩	♩	♩	♩	♩	♩
		♩	♩	♩	♩	♩	♩	♩
		♩	♩	♩	♩	♩	♩	♩
		♩	♩	♩	♩	♩	♩	♩
		♩	♩	♩	♩	♩	♩	♩
		♩	♩	♩	♩	♩	♩	♩
		♩	♩	♩	♩	♩	♩	♩
		♩	♩	♩	♩	♩	♩	♩

Practice Time (min)	Su	M	Tu	W	Th	F	Sa	Total

Weekly Recap

What went well this week:

What was challenging this week:

Questions/Comments:

Parent Signature: _____

Lesson Date: _____

Lesson Recap

In today's lesson, we worked on:

What went well:

What was challenging:

My main goal for the next week is:

Teacher comments:

Practice Plan

This week, I will practice _____ minutes per day for _____ days.

What to Practice:	What to Focus On:	Su M Tu W Th F Sa
		♩ ♩ ♩ ♩ ♩ ♩ ♩
		♩ ♩ ♩ ♩ ♩ ♩ ♩
		♩ ♩ ♩ ♩ ♩ ♩ ♩
		♩ ♩ ♩ ♩ ♩ ♩ ♩
		♩ ♩ ♩ ♩ ♩ ♩ ♩
		♩ ♩ ♩ ♩ ♩ ♩ ♩
		♩ ♩ ♩ ♩ ♩ ♩ ♩
		♩ ♩ ♩ ♩ ♩ ♩ ♩

Practice Time (min)	Su	M	Tu	W	Th	F	Sa	Total

Weekly Recap

What went well this week:

What was challenging this week:

Questions/Comments:

Parent Signature: _____

Lesson Date: _____

Lesson Recap

In today's lesson, we worked on:

What went well:

What was challenging:

My main goal for the next week is:

Teacher comments:

Practice Plan

This week, I will practice _____ minutes per day for _____ days.

What to Practice:	What to Focus On:	Su M Tu W Th F Sa
		♩ ♩ ♩ ♩ ♩ ♩ ♩
		♩ ♩ ♩ ♩ ♩ ♩ ♩
		♩ ♩ ♩ ♩ ♩ ♩ ♩
		♩ ♩ ♩ ♩ ♩ ♩ ♩
		♩ ♩ ♩ ♩ ♩ ♩ ♩
		♩ ♩ ♩ ♩ ♩ ♩ ♩
		♩ ♩ ♩ ♩ ♩ ♩ ♩
		♩ ♩ ♩ ♩ ♩ ♩ ♩

Practice Time (min)	Su	M	Tu	W	Th	F	Sa	Total

Weekly Recap

What went well this week:

What was challenging this week:

Questions/Comments:

Parent Signature: _____

Monthly Check–In

In the past month, I am proud that I...

In the past month, my biggest challenge was...

Just for Fun

You've worked hard this month! Take a break!

Directions: Color Mia playing the cello.

The Month Ahead

In the next month, I want to continue...

In the next month, I want to get better at...

In the next month, I want to learn...

Other notes:

Lesson Date: _____

Lesson Recap

In today's lesson, we worked on:

What went well:

What was challenging:

My main goal for the next week is:

Teacher comments:

Practice Plan

This week, I will practice _____ minutes per day for _____ days.

What to Practice:	What to Focus On:	Su	M	Tu	W	Th	F	Sa
		♩	♩	♩	♩	♩	♩	♩
		♩	♩	♩	♩	♩	♩	♩
		♩	♩	♩	♩	♩	♩	♩
		♩	♩	♩	♩	♩	♩	♩
		♩	♩	♩	♩	♩	♩	♩
		♩	♩	♩	♩	♩	♩	♩
		♩	♩	♩	♩	♩	♩	♩
		♩	♩	♩	♩	♩	♩	♩

Practice Time (min)	Su	M	Tu	W	Th	F	Sa	Total

Weekly Recap

What went well this week:

What was challenging this week:

Questions/Comments:

Parent Signature: _____

Lesson Date: _____

Lesson Recap

In today's lesson, we worked on:

What went well:

What was challenging:

My main goal for the next week is:

Teacher comments:

Practice Plan

This week, I will practice _____ minutes per day for _____ days.

What to Practice:	What to Focus On:	Su	M	Tu	W	Th	F	Sa
		♩	♩	♩	♩	♩	♩	♩
		♩	♩	♩	♩	♩	♩	♩
		♩	♩	♩	♩	♩	♩	♩
		♩	♩	♩	♩	♩	♩	♩
		♩	♩	♩	♩	♩	♩	♩
		♩	♩	♩	♩	♩	♩	♩
		♩	♩	♩	♩	♩	♩	♩
		♩	♩	♩	♩	♩	♩	♩

Practice Time (min)	Su	M	Tu	W	Th	F	Sa	Total

Weekly Recap

What went well this week:

What was challenging this week:

Questions/Comments:

Parent Signature: _____

Lesson Date: _____

Lesson Recap

In today's lesson, we worked on:

What went well:

What was challenging:

My main goal for the next week is:

Teacher comments:

Practice Plan

This week, I will practice _____ minutes per day for _____ days.

What to Practice:	What to Focus On:	Su M Tu W Th F Sa
		♩ ♩ ♩ ♩ ♩ ♩ ♩
		♩ ♩ ♩ ♩ ♩ ♩ ♩
		♩ ♩ ♩ ♩ ♩ ♩ ♩
		♩ ♩ ♩ ♩ ♩ ♩ ♩
		♩ ♩ ♩ ♩ ♩ ♩ ♩
		♩ ♩ ♩ ♩ ♩ ♩ ♩
		♩ ♩ ♩ ♩ ♩ ♩ ♩
		♩ ♩ ♩ ♩ ♩ ♩ ♩

Practice Time (min)	Su	M	Tu	W	Th	F	Sa	Total

Weekly Recap

What went well this week:

What was challenging this week:

Questions/Comments:

Parent Signature: _____

Lesson Date: _____

Lesson Recap

In today's lesson, we worked on:

What went well:

What was challenging:

My main goal for the next week is:

Teacher comments:

Practice Plan

This week, I will practice _____ minutes per day for _____ days.

What to Practice:	What to Focus On:	Su	M	Tu	W	Th	F	Sa
		♩	♩	♩	♩	♩	♩	♩
		♩	♩	♩	♩	♩	♩	♩
		♩	♩	♩	♩	♩	♩	♩
		♩	♩	♩	♩	♩	♩	♩
		♩	♩	♩	♩	♩	♩	♩
		♩	♩	♩	♩	♩	♩	♩
		♩	♩	♩	♩	♩	♩	♩
		♩	♩	♩	♩	♩	♩	♩

Practice Time (min)	Su	M	Tu	W	Th	F	Sa	Total

Weekly Recap

What went well this week:

What was challenging this week:

Questions/Comments:

Parent Signature: _____

Monthly Check-In

In the past month, I am proud that I...

In the past month, my biggest challenge was...

Just for Fun

You've worked hard this month! Take a break!

Directions: Find the musical terms from the word bank hidden in the puzzle below. The words may be written horizontally, vertically, or diagonally. (Answer key on p. 176)

```
C I F C T G K F M C S B
L P E T O T E M P O T A
E D G B P I T C H O R S
F O Y A R R B E N P A T
S O U N D L M Y R E S T
I K B E A T O A P L A D
L M F B N M R H Y T H M
M P L A Y E I H T C A S
U C U K E D N C K E L T
N O T E J G O K S V I F
O E L Y R D R T E A P T
K M U S I C A M U T R E
```

Word Bank

beat	clef	dynamics	key	music	note
pitch	play	rest	rhythm	sound	tempo

The Month Ahead

In the next month, I want to continue...

In the next month, I want to get better at...

In the next month, I want to learn...

Other notes:

Lesson Date: _____

Lesson Recap

In today's lesson, we worked on:

What went well:

What was challenging:

My main goal for the next week is:

Teacher comments:

Practice Plan

This week, I will practice _____ minutes per day for _____ days.

What to Practice:	What to Focus On:	Su M Tu W Th F Sa
		♩ ♩ ♩ ♩ ♩ ♩ ♩
		♩ ♩ ♩ ♩ ♩ ♩ ♩
		♩ ♩ ♩ ♩ ♩ ♩ ♩
		♩ ♩ ♩ ♩ ♩ ♩ ♩
		♩ ♩ ♩ ♩ ♩ ♩ ♩
		♩ ♩ ♩ ♩ ♩ ♩ ♩
		♩ ♩ ♩ ♩ ♩ ♩ ♩
		♩ ♩ ♩ ♩ ♩ ♩ ♩

Practice Time (min)

Su	M	Tu	W	Th	F	Sa	Total

Weekly Recap

What went well this week:

What was challenging this week:

Questions/Comments:

Parent Signature: _____

Lesson Date: _____

Lesson Recap

In today's lesson, we worked on:

What went well:

What was challenging:

My main goal for the next week is:

Teacher comments:

Practice Plan

This week, I will practice _____ minutes per day for _____ days.

What to Practice:	What to Focus On:	Su M Tu W Th F Sa
		♩ ♩ ♩ ♩ ♩ ♩ ♩
		♩ ♩ ♩ ♩ ♩ ♩ ♩
		♩ ♩ ♩ ♩ ♩ ♩ ♩
		♩ ♩ ♩ ♩ ♩ ♩ ♩
		♩ ♩ ♩ ♩ ♩ ♩ ♩
		♩ ♩ ♩ ♩ ♩ ♩ ♩
		♩ ♩ ♩ ♩ ♩ ♩ ♩
		♩ ♩ ♩ ♩ ♩ ♩ ♩

Practice Time (min)	Su	M	Tu	W	Th	F	Sa	Total

Weekly Recap

What went well this week:

What was challenging this week:

Questions/Comments:

Parent Signature: _____

Lesson Date: _____

Lesson Recap

In today's lesson, we worked on:

What went well:

What was challenging:

My main goal for the next week is:

Teacher comments:

Practice Plan

This week, I will practice _____ minutes per day for _____ days.

What to Practice:	What to Focus On:	Su M Tu W Th F Sa
		♩♩♩♩♩♩♩
		♩♩♩♩♩♩♩
		♩♩♩♩♩♩♩
		♩♩♩♩♩♩♩
		♩♩♩♩♩♩♩
		♩♩♩♩♩♩♩
		♩♩♩♩♩♩♩
		♩♩♩♩♩♩♩

Practice Time (min)	Su	M	Tu	W	Th	F	Sa	Total

Weekly Recap

What went well this week:

What was challenging this week:

Questions/Comments:

Parent Signature: _____

Lesson Date: _____

Lesson Recap

In today's lesson, we worked on:

What went well:

What was challenging:

My main goal for the next week is:

Teacher comments:

Practice Plan

This week, I will practice _____ minutes per day for _____ days.

What to Practice:	What to Focus On:	Su M Tu W Th F Sa
		♩ ♩ ♩ ♩ ♩ ♩ ♩
		♩ ♩ ♩ ♩ ♩ ♩ ♩
		♩ ♩ ♩ ♩ ♩ ♩ ♩
		♩ ♩ ♩ ♩ ♩ ♩ ♩
		♩ ♩ ♩ ♩ ♩ ♩ ♩
		♩ ♩ ♩ ♩ ♩ ♩ ♩
		♩ ♩ ♩ ♩ ♩ ♩ ♩
		♩ ♩ ♩ ♩ ♩ ♩ ♩

Practice Time (min)	Su	M	Tu	W	Th	F	Sa	Total

Weekly Recap

What went well this week:

What was challenging this week:

Questions/Comments:

Parent Signature: _____

Monthly Check-In

In the past month, I am proud that I...

In the past month, my biggest challenge was...

Just for Fun

You've worked hard this month! Take a break!

Directions: Find 6 differences between the two pictures below. (Answer key on p. 176)

The Month Ahead

In the next month, I want to continue...

In the next month, I want to get better at...

In the next month, I want to learn...

Other notes:

Lesson Date: _____

Lesson Recap

In today's lesson, we worked on:

What went well:

What was challenging:

My main goal for the next week is:

Teacher comments:

Practice Plan

This week, I will practice _____ minutes per day for _____ days.

What to Practice:	What to Focus On:	Su	M	Tu	W	Th	F	Sa
		♩	♩	♩	♩	♩	♩	♩
		♩	♩	♩	♩	♩	♩	♩
		♩	♩	♩	♩	♩	♩	♩
		♩	♩	♩	♩	♩	♩	♩
		♩	♩	♩	♩	♩	♩	♩
		♩	♩	♩	♩	♩	♩	♩
		♩	♩	♩	♩	♩	♩	♩
		♩	♩	♩	♩	♩	♩	♩

Practice Time (min)	Su	M	Tu	W	Th	F	Sa	Total

Weekly Recap

What went well this week:

What was challenging this week:

Questions/Comments:

Parent Signature: _____

Lesson Date: _____

Lesson Recap

In today's lesson, we worked on:

What went well:

What was challenging:

My main goal for the next week is:

Teacher comments:

Practice Plan

This week, I will practice _____ minutes per day for _____ days.

What to Practice:	What to Focus On:	Su M Tu W Th F Sa
		♩ ♩ ♩ ♩ ♩ ♩ ♩
		♩ ♩ ♩ ♩ ♩ ♩ ♩
		♩ ♩ ♩ ♩ ♩ ♩ ♩
		♩ ♩ ♩ ♩ ♩ ♩ ♩
		♩ ♩ ♩ ♩ ♩ ♩ ♩
		♩ ♩ ♩ ♩ ♩ ♩ ♩
		♩ ♩ ♩ ♩ ♩ ♩ ♩
		♩ ♩ ♩ ♩ ♩ ♩ ♩

Practice Time (min)	Su	M	Tu	W	Th	F	Sa	Total

Weekly Recap

What went well this week:

What was challenging this week:

Questions/Comments:

Parent Signature: _____

Lesson Date: _____

Lesson Recap

In today's lesson, we worked on:

What went well:

What was challenging:

My main goal for the next week is:

Teacher comments:

Practice Plan

This week, I will practice _____ minutes per day for _____ days.

What to Practice:	What to Focus On:	Su M Tu W Th F Sa
		♩ ♩ ♩ ♩ ♩ ♩ ♩
		♩ ♩ ♩ ♩ ♩ ♩ ♩
		♩ ♩ ♩ ♩ ♩ ♩ ♩
		♩ ♩ ♩ ♩ ♩ ♩ ♩
		♩ ♩ ♩ ♩ ♩ ♩ ♩
		♩ ♩ ♩ ♩ ♩ ♩ ♩
		♩ ♩ ♩ ♩ ♩ ♩ ♩
		♩ ♩ ♩ ♩ ♩ ♩ ♩

Practice Time (min)	Su	M	Tu	W	Th	F	Sa	Total

Weekly Recap

What went well this week:

What was challenging this week:

Questions/Comments:

Parent Signature: _____

Lesson Date: _____

Lesson Recap

In today's lesson, we worked on:

What went well:

What was challenging:

My main goal for the next week is:

Teacher comments:

Practice Plan

This week, I will practice _____ minutes per day for _____ days.

What to Practice:	What to Focus On:	Su M Tu W Th F Sa
		♩♩♩♩♩♩♩
		♩♩♩♩♩♩♩
		♩♩♩♩♩♩♩
		♩♩♩♩♩♩♩
		♩♩♩♩♩♩♩
		♩♩♩♩♩♩♩
		♩♩♩♩♩♩♩
		♩♩♩♩♩♩♩

Practice Time (min)	Su	M	Tu	W	Th	F	Sa	Total

Weekly Recap

What went well this week:

What was challenging this week:

Questions/Comments:

Parent Signature: _____

Monthly Check-In

In the past month, I am proud that I...

In the past month, my biggest challenge was...

Just for Fun

You've worked hard this month! Take a break!

Directions: Write the letter name of each note on the lines below to spell the words. Then fill in the words on the crossword puzzle. 1 Down is solved for you. (Answer key on p. 177)

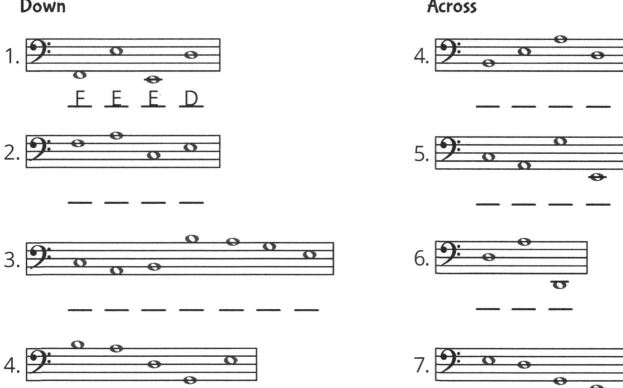

The Month Ahead

In the next month, I want to continue...

In the next month, I want to get better at...

In the next month, I want to learn...

Other notes:

Lesson Date: _____

Lesson Recap

In today's lesson, we worked on:

What went well:

What was challenging:

My main goal for the next week is:

Teacher comments:

Practice Plan

This week, I will practice _____ minutes per day for _____ days.

What to Practice:	What to Focus On:	Su M Tu W Th F Sa
		♩ ♩ ♩ ♩ ♩ ♩ ♩
		♩ ♩ ♩ ♩ ♩ ♩ ♩
		♩ ♩ ♩ ♩ ♩ ♩ ♩
		♩ ♩ ♩ ♩ ♩ ♩ ♩
		♩ ♩ ♩ ♩ ♩ ♩ ♩
		♩ ♩ ♩ ♩ ♩ ♩ ♩
		♩ ♩ ♩ ♩ ♩ ♩ ♩
		♩ ♩ ♩ ♩ ♩ ♩ ♩

Practice Time (min)	Su	M	Tu	W	Th	F	Sa	Total

Weekly Recap

What went well this week:

What was challenging this week:

Questions/Comments:

Parent Signature: _____

Lesson Date: _____

Lesson Recap

In today's lesson, we worked on:

What went well:

What was challenging:

My main goal for the next week is:

Teacher comments:

Practice Plan

This week, I will practice _____ minutes per day for _____ days.

What to Practice:	What to Focus On:	Su M Tu W Th F Sa
		♩ ♩ ♩ ♩ ♩ ♩ ♩
		♩ ♩ ♩ ♩ ♩ ♩ ♩
		♩ ♩ ♩ ♩ ♩ ♩ ♩
		♩ ♩ ♩ ♩ ♩ ♩ ♩
		♩ ♩ ♩ ♩ ♩ ♩ ♩
		♩ ♩ ♩ ♩ ♩ ♩ ♩
		♩ ♩ ♩ ♩ ♩ ♩ ♩
		♩ ♩ ♩ ♩ ♩ ♩ ♩

Practice Time (min)	Su	M	Tu	W	Th	F	Sa	Total

Weekly Recap

What went well this week:

What was challenging this week:

Questions/Comments:

Parent Signature: _____

Lesson Date: _____

Lesson Recap

In today's lesson, we worked on:

What went well:

What was challenging:

My main goal for the next week is:

Teacher comments:

Practice Plan

This week, I will practice _____ minutes per day for _____ days.

What to Practice:	What to Focus On:	Su	M	Tu	W	Th	F	Sa
		♩	♩	♩	♩	♩	♩	♩
		♩	♩	♩	♩	♩	♩	♩
		♩	♩	♩	♩	♩	♩	♩
		♩	♩	♩	♩	♩	♩	♩
		♩	♩	♩	♩	♩	♩	♩
		♩	♩	♩	♩	♩	♩	♩
		♩	♩	♩	♩	♩	♩	♩
		♩	♩	♩	♩	♩	♩	♩

Practice Time (min)	Su	M	Tu	W	Th	F	Sa	Total

Weekly Recap

What went well this week:

What was challenging this week:

Questions/Comments:

Parent Signature: _____

Lesson Date: _____

Lesson Recap

In today's lesson, we worked on:

What went well:

What was challenging:

My main goal for the next week is:

Teacher comments:

Practice Plan

This week, I will practice _____ minutes per day for _____ days.

What to Practice:	What to Focus On:	Su M Tu W Th F Sa
		♩ ♩ ♩ ♩ ♩ ♩ ♩
		♩ ♩ ♩ ♩ ♩ ♩ ♩
		♩ ♩ ♩ ♩ ♩ ♩ ♩
		♩ ♩ ♩ ♩ ♩ ♩ ♩
		♩ ♩ ♩ ♩ ♩ ♩ ♩
		♩ ♩ ♩ ♩ ♩ ♩ ♩
		♩ ♩ ♩ ♩ ♩ ♩ ♩
		♩ ♩ ♩ ♩ ♩ ♩ ♩

Practice Time (min)	Su	M	Tu	W	Th	F	Sa	Total

Weekly Recap

What went well this week:

What was challenging this week:

Questions/Comments:

Parent Signature: _____

Monthly Check-In

In the past month, I am proud that I...

In the past month, my biggest challenge was...

Just for Fun

You've worked hard this month! Take a break!

Directions: Help Ava find her way through the maze to the stage in time for her big recital! (Answer key on p. 177)

The Month Ahead

In the next month, I want to continue…

In the next month, I want to get better at…

In the next month, I want to learn…

Other notes:

Lesson Date: _____

Lesson Recap

In today's lesson, we worked on:

What went well:

What was challenging:

My main goal for the next week is:

Teacher comments:

Practice Plan

This week, I will practice _____ minutes per day for _____ days.

What to Practice:	What to Focus On:	Su M Tu W Th F Sa
		♩ ♩ ♩ ♩ ♩ ♩ ♩
		♩ ♩ ♩ ♩ ♩ ♩ ♩
		♩ ♩ ♩ ♩ ♩ ♩ ♩
		♩ ♩ ♩ ♩ ♩ ♩ ♩
		♩ ♩ ♩ ♩ ♩ ♩ ♩
		♩ ♩ ♩ ♩ ♩ ♩ ♩
		♩ ♩ ♩ ♩ ♩ ♩ ♩
		♩ ♩ ♩ ♩ ♩ ♩ ♩

Practice Time (min)	Su	M	Tu	W	Th	F	Sa	Total

Weekly Recap

What went well this week:

What was challenging this week:

Questions/Comments:

Parent Signature: _____

Lesson Date: _____

Lesson Recap

In today's lesson, we worked on:

What went well:

What was challenging:

My main goal for the next week is:

Teacher comments:

Practice Plan

This week, I will practice _____ minutes per day for _____ days.

What to Practice:	What to Focus On:	Su	M	Tu	W	Th	F	Sa
		♩	♩	♩	♩	♩	♩	♩
		♩	♩	♩	♩	♩	♩	♩
		♩	♩	♩	♩	♩	♩	♩
		♩	♩	♩	♩	♩	♩	♩
		♩	♩	♩	♩	♩	♩	♩
		♩	♩	♩	♩	♩	♩	♩
		♩	♩	♩	♩	♩	♩	♩
		♩	♩	♩	♩	♩	♩	♩

Practice Time (min)	Su	M	Tu	W	Th	F	Sa	Total

Weekly Recap

What went well this week:

What was challenging this week:

Questions/Comments:

Parent Signature: _____

Lesson Date: _____

Lesson Recap

In today's lesson, we worked on:

What went well:

What was challenging:

My main goal for the next week is:

Teacher comments:

Practice Plan

This week, I will practice _____ minutes per day for _____ days.

What to Practice:	What to Focus On:	Su M Tu W Th F Sa
		♩ ♩ ♩ ♩ ♩ ♩ ♩
		♩ ♩ ♩ ♩ ♩ ♩ ♩
		♩ ♩ ♩ ♩ ♩ ♩ ♩
		♩ ♩ ♩ ♩ ♩ ♩ ♩
		♩ ♩ ♩ ♩ ♩ ♩ ♩
		♩ ♩ ♩ ♩ ♩ ♩ ♩
		♩ ♩ ♩ ♩ ♩ ♩ ♩
		♩ ♩ ♩ ♩ ♩ ♩ ♩

Practice Time (min)	Su	M	Tu	W	Th	F	Sa	Total

Weekly Recap

What went well this week:

What was challenging this week:

Questions/Comments:

Parent Signature: _____

Lesson Date: _____

Lesson Recap

In today's lesson, we worked on:

What went well:

What was challenging:

My main goal for the next week is:

Teacher comments:

Practice Plan

This week, I will practice _____ minutes per day for _____ days.

What to Practice:	What to Focus On:	Su	M	Tu	W	Th	F	Sa
		♩	♩	♩	♩	♩	♩	♩
		♩	♩	♩	♩	♩	♩	♩
		♩	♩	♩	♩	♩	♩	♩
		♩	♩	♩	♩	♩	♩	♩
		♩	♩	♩	♩	♩	♩	♩
		♩	♩	♩	♩	♩	♩	♩
		♩	♩	♩	♩	♩	♩	♩
		♩	♩	♩	♩	♩	♩	♩

Practice Time (min)	Su	M	Tu	W	Th	F	Sa	Total

Weekly Recap

What went well this week:

What was challenging this week:

Questions/Comments:

Parent Signature: _____

Monthly Check-In

In the past month, I am proud that I…

In the past month, my biggest challenge was…

Just for Fun

You've worked hard this month! Take a break!

Directions: Unscramble the letters to spell musical terms. (Answer key on p. 178)

Ex:	S M I U C	MUSIC
1.	L C O E L	_____
2.	C R P T E A C I	_____
3.	S O N T E	_____
4.	H Y H T R M	_____
5.	S R E T	_____
6.	G I B W N O	_____
7.	E S C S A L	_____
8.	P H S R A	_____
9.	M O T P E	_____
10.	I S M A C D Y N	_____

The Month Ahead

In the next month, I want to continue...

In the next month, I want to get better at...

In the next month, I want to learn...

Other notes:

Lesson Date: _____

Lesson Recap

In today's lesson, we worked on:

What went well:

What was challenging:

My main goal for the next week is:

Teacher comments:

Practice Plan

This week, I will practice _____ minutes per day for _____ days.

What to Practice:	What to Focus On:	Su M Tu W Th F Sa
		♩ ♩ ♩ ♩ ♩ ♩ ♩
		♩ ♩ ♩ ♩ ♩ ♩ ♩
		♩ ♩ ♩ ♩ ♩ ♩ ♩
		♩ ♩ ♩ ♩ ♩ ♩ ♩
		♩ ♩ ♩ ♩ ♩ ♩ ♩
		♩ ♩ ♩ ♩ ♩ ♩ ♩
		♩ ♩ ♩ ♩ ♩ ♩ ♩
		♩ ♩ ♩ ♩ ♩ ♩ ♩

Practice Time (min)	Su	M	Tu	W	Th	F	Sa	Total

Weekly Recap

What went well this week:

What was challenging this week:

Questions/Comments:

Parent Signature: _____

Lesson Date: _____

Lesson Recap

In today's lesson, we worked on:

What went well:

What was challenging:

My main goal for the next week is:

Teacher comments:

Practice Plan

This week, I will practice _____ minutes per day for _____ days.

What to Practice:	What to Focus On:	Su	M	Tu	W	Th	F	Sa
		♩	♩	♩	♩	♩	♩	♩
		♩	♩	♩	♩	♩	♩	♩
		♩	♩	♩	♩	♩	♩	♩
		♩	♩	♩	♩	♩	♩	♩
		♩	♩	♩	♩	♩	♩	♩
		♩	♩	♩	♩	♩	♩	♩
		♩	♩	♩	♩	♩	♩	♩
		♩	♩	♩	♩	♩	♩	♩

Practice Time (min)	Su	M	Tu	W	Th	F	Sa	Total

Weekly Recap

What went well this week:

What was challenging this week:

Questions/Comments:

Parent Signature: _____

Lesson Date: _____

Lesson Recap

In today's lesson, we worked on:

What went well:

What was challenging:

My main goal for the next week is:

Teacher comments:

Practice Plan

This week, I will practice _____ minutes per day for _____ days.

What to Practice:	What to Focus On:	Su	M	Tu	W	Th	F	Sa
		♩	♩	♩	♩	♩	♩	♩
		♩	♩	♩	♩	♩	♩	♩
		♩	♩	♩	♩	♩	♩	♩
		♩	♩	♩	♩	♩	♩	♩
		♩	♩	♩	♩	♩	♩	♩
		♩	♩	♩	♩	♩	♩	♩
		♩	♩	♩	♩	♩	♩	♩
		♩	♩	♩	♩	♩	♩	♩

Practice Time (min)	Su	M	Tu	W	Th	F	Sa	Total

Weekly Recap

What went well this week:

What was challenging this week:

Questions/Comments:

Parent Signature: _____

Lesson Date: _____

Lesson Recap

In today's lesson, we worked on:

What went well:

What was challenging:

My main goal for the next week is:

Teacher comments:

Practice Plan

This week, I will practice _____ minutes per day for _____ days.

What to Practice:	What to Focus On:	Su M Tu W Th F Sa
		♩ ♩ ♩ ♩ ♩ ♩ ♩
		♩ ♩ ♩ ♩ ♩ ♩ ♩
		♩ ♩ ♩ ♩ ♩ ♩ ♩
		♩ ♩ ♩ ♩ ♩ ♩ ♩
		♩ ♩ ♩ ♩ ♩ ♩ ♩
		♩ ♩ ♩ ♩ ♩ ♩ ♩
		♩ ♩ ♩ ♩ ♩ ♩ ♩
		♩ ♩ ♩ ♩ ♩ ♩ ♩

Practice Time (min)	Su	M	Tu	W	Th	F	Sa	Total

Weekly Recap

What went well this week:

What was challenging this week:

Questions/Comments:

Parent Signature: _____

Monthly Check-In

In the past month, I am proud that I...

In the past month, my biggest challenge was...

Just for Fun

You've worked hard this month! Take a break!

Directions: Use the key below to color the shapes containing each symbol to reveal the picture.

Key

Bass clef = green   Natural = blue   Sharp = black   Flat = purple

Eighth note = orange   Quarter note = yellow   Half note = pink

The Month Ahead

In the next month, I want to continue…

In the next month, I want to get better at…

In the next month, I want to learn…

Other notes:

Lesson Date: _____

Lesson Recap

In today's lesson, we worked on:

What went well:

What was challenging:

My main goal for the next week is:

Teacher comments:

Practice Plan

This week, I will practice _____ minutes per day for _____ days.

What to Practice:	What to Focus On:	Su M Tu W Th F Sa
		♩ ♩ ♩ ♩ ♩ ♩ ♩
		♩ ♩ ♩ ♩ ♩ ♩ ♩
		♩ ♩ ♩ ♩ ♩ ♩ ♩
		♩ ♩ ♩ ♩ ♩ ♩ ♩
		♩ ♩ ♩ ♩ ♩ ♩ ♩
		♩ ♩ ♩ ♩ ♩ ♩ ♩
		♩ ♩ ♩ ♩ ♩ ♩ ♩
		♩ ♩ ♩ ♩ ♩ ♩ ♩

Practice Time (min)	Su	M	Tu	W	Th	F	Sa	Total

Weekly Recap

What went well this week:

What was challenging this week:

Questions/Comments:

Parent Signature: _____

Lesson Date: _____

Lesson Recap

In today's lesson, we worked on:

What went well:

What was challenging:

My main goal for the next week is:

Teacher comments:

Practice Plan

This week, I will practice _____ minutes per day for _____ days.

What to Practice:	What to Focus On:	Su	M	Tu	W	Th	F	Sa
		♩	♩	♩	♩	♩	♩	♩
		♩	♩	♩	♩	♩	♩	♩
		♩	♩	♩	♩	♩	♩	♩
		♩	♩	♩	♩	♩	♩	♩
		♩	♩	♩	♩	♩	♩	♩
		♩	♩	♩	♩	♩	♩	♩
		♩	♩	♩	♩	♩	♩	♩
		♩	♩	♩	♩	♩	♩	♩

Practice Time (min)	Su	M	Tu	W	Th	F	Sa	Total

Weekly Recap

What went well this week:

What was challenging this week:

Questions/Comments:

Parent Signature: _____

Lesson Date: _____

Lesson Recap

In today's lesson, we worked on:

What went well:

What was challenging:

My main goal for the next week is:

Teacher comments:

Practice Plan

This week, I will practice _____ minutes per day for _____ days.

What to Practice:	What to Focus On:	Su M Tu W Th F Sa
		♩ ♩ ♩ ♩ ♩ ♩ ♩
		♩ ♩ ♩ ♩ ♩ ♩ ♩
		♩ ♩ ♩ ♩ ♩ ♩ ♩
		♩ ♩ ♩ ♩ ♩ ♩ ♩
		♩ ♩ ♩ ♩ ♩ ♩ ♩
		♩ ♩ ♩ ♩ ♩ ♩ ♩
		♩ ♩ ♩ ♩ ♩ ♩ ♩
		♩ ♩ ♩ ♩ ♩ ♩ ♩

Practice Time (min)	Su	M	Tu	W	Th	F	Sa	Total

Weekly Recap

What went well this week:

What was challenging this week:

Questions/Comments:

Parent Signature: _____

Lesson Date: _____

Lesson Recap

In today's lesson, we worked on:

What went well:

What was challenging:

My main goal for the next week is:

Teacher comments:

Practice Plan

This week, I will practice _____ minutes per day for _____ days.

What to Practice:	What to Focus On:	Su M Tu W Th F Sa
		♩ ♩ ♩ ♩ ♩ ♩ ♩
		♩ ♩ ♩ ♩ ♩ ♩ ♩
		♩ ♩ ♩ ♩ ♩ ♩ ♩
		♩ ♩ ♩ ♩ ♩ ♩ ♩
		♩ ♩ ♩ ♩ ♩ ♩ ♩
		♩ ♩ ♩ ♩ ♩ ♩ ♩
		♩ ♩ ♩ ♩ ♩ ♩ ♩
		♩ ♩ ♩ ♩ ♩ ♩ ♩

Practice Time (min)	Su	M	Tu	W	Th	F	Sa	Total

Weekly Recap

What went well this week:

What was challenging this week:

Questions/Comments:

Parent Signature: _____

Monthly Check—In

In the past month, I am proud that I...

In the past month, my biggest challenge was...

Just for Fun

You've worked hard this month! Take a break!

Directions: Find and circle the musical terms represented by each of the symbols hidden in the letters below. The terms may be written horizontally, vertically, or diagonally, and they may be more than one word. The first one is solved for you. (Answer key on p. 178)

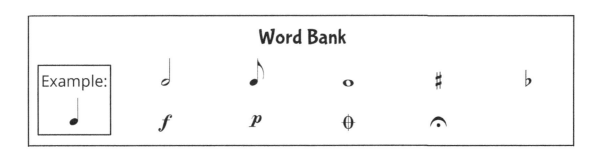

The Month Ahead

In the next month, I want to continue...

In the next month, I want to get better at...

In the next month, I want to learn...

Other notes:

Lesson Date: _____

Lesson Recap

In today's lesson, we worked on:

What went well:

What was challenging:

My main goal for the next week is:

Teacher comments:

Practice Plan

This week, I will practice _____ minutes per day for _____ days.

What to Practice:	What to Focus On:	Su M Tu W Th F Sa
		♩ ♩ ♩ ♩ ♩ ♩ ♩
		♩ ♩ ♩ ♩ ♩ ♩ ♩
		♩ ♩ ♩ ♩ ♩ ♩ ♩
		♩ ♩ ♩ ♩ ♩ ♩ ♩
		♩ ♩ ♩ ♩ ♩ ♩ ♩
		♩ ♩ ♩ ♩ ♩ ♩ ♩
		♩ ♩ ♩ ♩ ♩ ♩ ♩
		♩ ♩ ♩ ♩ ♩ ♩ ♩

Practice Time (min)	Su	M	Tu	W	Th	F	Sa	Total

Weekly Recap

What went well this week:

What was challenging this week:

Questions/Comments:

Parent Signature: _____

Lesson Date: _____

Lesson Recap

In today's lesson, we worked on:

What went well:

What was challenging:

My main goal for the next week is:

Teacher comments:

Practice Plan

This week, I will practice _____ minutes per day for _____ days.

What to Practice:	What to Focus On:	Su M Tu W Th F Sa
		♩ ♩ ♩ ♩ ♩ ♩ ♩
		♩ ♩ ♩ ♩ ♩ ♩ ♩
		♩ ♩ ♩ ♩ ♩ ♩ ♩
		♩ ♩ ♩ ♩ ♩ ♩ ♩
		♩ ♩ ♩ ♩ ♩ ♩ ♩
		♩ ♩ ♩ ♩ ♩ ♩ ♩
		♩ ♩ ♩ ♩ ♩ ♩ ♩
		♩ ♩ ♩ ♩ ♩ ♩ ♩

Practice Time (min)	Su	M	Tu	W	Th	F	Sa	Total

Weekly Recap

What went well this week:

What was challenging this week:

Questions/Comments:

Parent Signature: _____

Lesson Date: _____

Lesson Recap

In today's lesson, we worked on:

What went well:

What was challenging:

My main goal for the next week is:

Teacher comments:

Practice Plan

This week, I will practice _____ minutes per day for _____ days.

What to Practice:	What to Focus On:	Su M Tu W Th F Sa
		♩ ♩ ♩ ♩ ♩ ♩ ♩
		♩ ♩ ♩ ♩ ♩ ♩ ♩
		♩ ♩ ♩ ♩ ♩ ♩ ♩
		♩ ♩ ♩ ♩ ♩ ♩ ♩
		♩ ♩ ♩ ♩ ♩ ♩ ♩
		♩ ♩ ♩ ♩ ♩ ♩ ♩
		♩ ♩ ♩ ♩ ♩ ♩ ♩
		♩ ♩ ♩ ♩ ♩ ♩ ♩

Practice Time (min) | Su | M | Tu | W | Th | F | Sa | Total

Weekly Recap

What went well this week:

What was challenging this week:

Questions/Comments:

Parent Signature: _____

Lesson Date: _____

Lesson Recap

In today's lesson, we worked on:

What went well:

What was challenging:

My main goal for the next week is:

Teacher comments:

Practice Plan

This week, I will practice _____ minutes per day for _____ days.

What to Practice:	What to Focus On:	Su M Tu W Th F Sa
		♩♩♩♩♩♩♩
		♩♩♩♩♩♩♩
		♩♩♩♩♩♩♩
		♩♩♩♩♩♩♩
		♩♩♩♩♩♩♩
		♩♩♩♩♩♩♩
		♩♩♩♩♩♩♩
		♩♩♩♩♩♩♩

Practice Time (min)	Su	M	Tu	W	Th	F	Sa	Total

Weekly Recap

What went well this week:

What was challenging this week:

Questions/Comments:

Parent Signature: _____

Monthly Check-In

In the past month, I am proud that I...

In the past month, my biggest challenge was...

Just for Fun

You've worked hard this month! Take a break!

Directions: Connect the dots in order from 1 to 61 to complete the picture. Then, color it in.

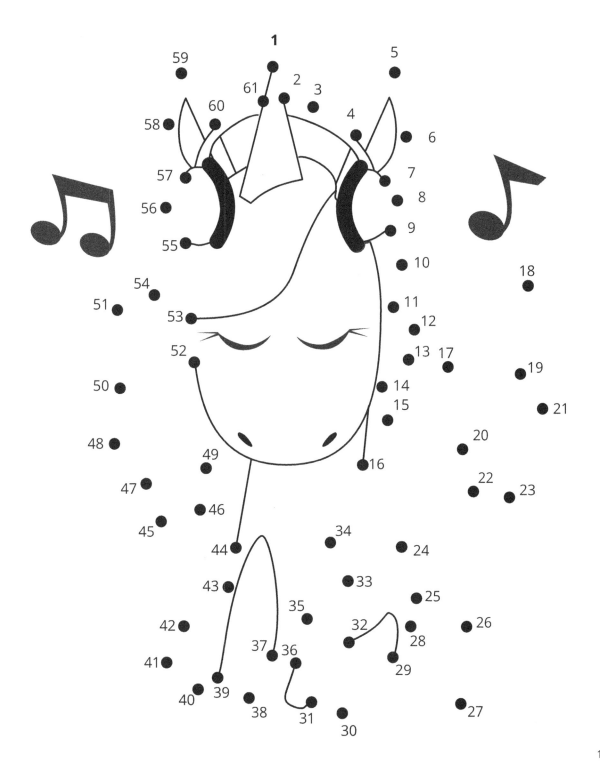

The Month Ahead

In the next month, I want to continue...

In the next month, I want to get better at...

In the next month, I want to learn...

Other notes:

Lesson Date: _____

Lesson Recap

In today's lesson, we worked on:

What went well:

What was challenging:

My main goal for the next week is:

Teacher comments:

Practice Plan

This week, I will practice _____ minutes per day for _____ days.

What to Practice:	What to Focus On:	Su M Tu W Th F Sa
		♩ ♩ ♩ ♩ ♩ ♩ ♩
		♩ ♩ ♩ ♩ ♩ ♩ ♩
		♩ ♩ ♩ ♩ ♩ ♩ ♩
		♩ ♩ ♩ ♩ ♩ ♩ ♩
		♩ ♩ ♩ ♩ ♩ ♩ ♩
		♩ ♩ ♩ ♩ ♩ ♩ ♩
		♩ ♩ ♩ ♩ ♩ ♩ ♩
		♩ ♩ ♩ ♩ ♩ ♩ ♩

Practice Time (min)	Su	M	Tu	W	Th	F	Sa	Total

Weekly Recap

What went well this week:

What was challenging this week:

Questions/Comments:

Parent Signature: _____

Lesson Date: _____

Lesson Recap

In today's lesson, we worked on:

What went well:

What was challenging:

My main goal for the next week is:

Teacher comments:

Practice Plan

This week, I will practice _____ minutes per day for _____ days.

What to Practice:	What to Focus On:	Su M Tu W Th F Sa
		♩♩♩♩♩♩♩
		♩♩♩♩♩♩♩
		♩♩♩♩♩♩♩
		♩♩♩♩♩♩♩
		♩♩♩♩♩♩♩
		♩♩♩♩♩♩♩
		♩♩♩♩♩♩♩
		♩♩♩♩♩♩♩

Practice Time (min) | Su | M | Tu | W | Th | F | Sa | Total

Weekly Recap

What went well this week:

What was challenging this week:

Questions/Comments:

Parent Signature: _____

Lesson Date: _____

Lesson Recap

In today's lesson, we worked on:

What went well:

What was challenging:

My main goal for the next week is:

Teacher comments:

Practice Plan

This week, I will practice _____ minutes per day for _____ days.

What to Practice:	What to Focus On:	Su	M	Tu	W	Th	F	Sa
		♪	♪	♪	♪	♪	♪	♪
		♪	♪	♪	♪	♪	♪	♪
		♪	♪	♪	♪	♪	♪	♪
		♪	♪	♪	♪	♪	♪	♪
		♪	♪	♪	♪	♪	♪	♪
		♪	♪	♪	♪	♪	♪	♪
		♪	♪	♪	♪	♪	♪	♪
		♪	♪	♪	♪	♪	♪	♪

Practice Time (min)	Su	M	Tu	W	Th	F	Sa	Total

Weekly Recap

What went well this week:

What was challenging this week:

Questions/Comments:

Parent Signature: _____

Lesson Date: _____

Lesson Recap

In today's lesson, we worked on:

What went well:

What was challenging:

My main goal for the next week is:

Teacher comments:

Practice Plan

This week, I will practice _____ minutes per day for _____ days.

What to Practice:	What to Focus On:	Su M Tu W Th F Sa
		♩ ♩ ♩ ♩ ♩ ♩ ♩
		♩ ♩ ♩ ♩ ♩ ♩ ♩
		♩ ♩ ♩ ♩ ♩ ♩ ♩
		♩ ♩ ♩ ♩ ♩ ♩ ♩
		♩ ♩ ♩ ♩ ♩ ♩ ♩
		♩ ♩ ♩ ♩ ♩ ♩ ♩
		♩ ♩ ♩ ♩ ♩ ♩ ♩
		♩ ♩ ♩ ♩ ♩ ♩ ♩

Practice Time (min)	Su	M	Tu	W	Th	F	Sa	Total

Weekly Recap

What went well this week:

What was challenging this week:

Questions/Comments:

Parent Signature: _____

Monthly Check-In

In the past month, I am proud that I...

In the past month, my biggest challenge was...

Just for Fun

You've worked hard this month! Take a break!

Directions: In the code shown below, each letter of the alphabet is represented by a different musical symbol. Use this to fill in the correct letters in the blanks and reveal the musical code names of famous composers. The first one is solved for you. (Answer key on p. 179)

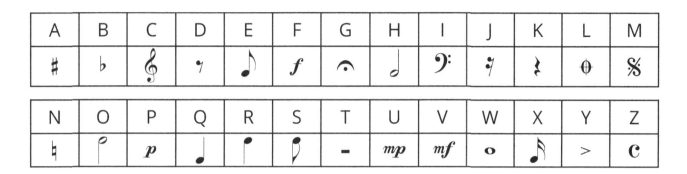

Now you try it! Write your name in musical code below.

The Month Ahead

In the next month, I want to continue...

In the next month, I want to get better at...

In the next month, I want to learn...

Other notes:

Lesson Date: _____

Lesson Recap

In today's lesson, we worked on:

What went well:

What was challenging:

My main goal for the next week is:

Teacher comments:

Practice Plan

This week, I will practice _____ minutes per day for _____ days.

What to Practice:	What to Focus On:	Su	M	Tu	W	Th	F	Sa
		♩	♩	♩	♩	♩	♩	♩
		♩	♩	♩	♩	♩	♩	♩
		♩	♩	♩	♩	♩	♩	♩
		♩	♩	♩	♩	♩	♩	♩
		♩	♩	♩	♩	♩	♩	♩
		♩	♩	♩	♩	♩	♩	♩
		♩	♩	♩	♩	♩	♩	♩
		♩	♩	♩	♩	♩	♩	♩

Practice Time (min)	Su	M	Tu	W	Th	F	Sa	Total

Weekly Recap

What went well this week:

What was challenging this week:

Questions/Comments:

Parent Signature: _____

Lesson Date: _____

Lesson Recap

In today's lesson, we worked on:

What went well:

What was challenging:

My main goal for the next week is:

Teacher comments:

Practice Plan

This week, I will practice _____ minutes per day for _____ days.

What to Practice:	What to Focus On:	Su M Tu W Th F Sa
		♩ ♩ ♩ ♩ ♩ ♩ ♩
		♩ ♩ ♩ ♩ ♩ ♩ ♩
		♩ ♩ ♩ ♩ ♩ ♩ ♩
		♩ ♩ ♩ ♩ ♩ ♩ ♩
		♩ ♩ ♩ ♩ ♩ ♩ ♩
		♩ ♩ ♩ ♩ ♩ ♩ ♩
		♩ ♩ ♩ ♩ ♩ ♩ ♩
		♩ ♩ ♩ ♩ ♩ ♩ ♩

Practice Time (min)	Su	M	Tu	W	Th	F	Sa	Total

Weekly Recap

What went well this week:

What was challenging this week:

Questions/Comments:

Parent Signature: _____

Lesson Date: _____

Lesson Recap

In today's lesson, we worked on:

What went well:

What was challenging:

My main goal for the next week is:

Teacher comments:

Practice Plan

This week, I will practice _____ minutes per day for _____ days.

What to Practice:	What to Focus On:	Su M Tu W Th F Sa
		♩ ♩ ♩ ♩ ♩ ♩ ♩
		♩ ♩ ♩ ♩ ♩ ♩ ♩
		♩ ♩ ♩ ♩ ♩ ♩ ♩
		♩ ♩ ♩ ♩ ♩ ♩ ♩
		♩ ♩ ♩ ♩ ♩ ♩ ♩
		♩ ♩ ♩ ♩ ♩ ♩ ♩
		♩ ♩ ♩ ♩ ♩ ♩ ♩
		♩ ♩ ♩ ♩ ♩ ♩ ♩

Practice Time (min)	Su	M	Tu	W	Th	F	Sa	Total

Weekly Recap

What went well this week:

What was challenging this week:

Questions/Comments:

Parent Signature: _____

Lesson Date: _____

Lesson Recap

In today's lesson, we worked on:

What went well:

What was challenging:

My main goal for the next week is:

Teacher comments:

Practice Plan

This week, I will practice _____ minutes per day for _____ days.

What to Practice:	What to Focus On:	Su M Tu W Th F Sa
		♩ ♩ ♩ ♩ ♩ ♩ ♩
		♩ ♩ ♩ ♩ ♩ ♩ ♩
		♩ ♩ ♩ ♩ ♩ ♩ ♩
		♩ ♩ ♩ ♩ ♩ ♩ ♩
		♩ ♩ ♩ ♩ ♩ ♩ ♩
		♩ ♩ ♩ ♩ ♩ ♩ ♩
		♩ ♩ ♩ ♩ ♩ ♩ ♩
		♩ ♩ ♩ ♩ ♩ ♩ ♩

Practice Time (min)	Su	M	Tu	W	Th	F	Sa	Total

Weekly Recap

What went well this week:

What was challenging this week:

Questions/Comments:

Parent Signature: _____

Monthly Check-In

In the past month, I am proud that I...

In the past month, my biggest challenge was...

Just for Fun

You've worked hard this month! Take a break!

Directions: Name each note shown on the staves below. Then, color the areas of the picture labeled with that letter with the color shown.

Red

Brown

Purple

Pink

Blue

Gray

143

The Month Ahead

In the next month, I want to continue...

In the next month, I want to get better at...

In the next month, I want to learn...

Other notes:

Lesson Date: _____

Lesson Recap

In today's lesson, we worked on:

What went well:

What was challenging:

My main goal for the next week is:

Teacher comments:

Practice Plan

This week, I will practice _____ minutes per day for _____ days.

What to Practice:	What to Focus On:	Su M Tu W Th F Sa
		♩ ♩ ♩ ♩ ♩ ♩ ♩
		♩ ♩ ♩ ♩ ♩ ♩ ♩
		♩ ♩ ♩ ♩ ♩ ♩ ♩
		♩ ♩ ♩ ♩ ♩ ♩ ♩
		♩ ♩ ♩ ♩ ♩ ♩ ♩
		♩ ♩ ♩ ♩ ♩ ♩ ♩
		♩ ♩ ♩ ♩ ♩ ♩ ♩
		♩ ♩ ♩ ♩ ♩ ♩ ♩

Practice Time (min)	Su	M	Tu	W	Th	F	Sa	Total

Weekly Recap

What went well this week:

What was challenging this week:

Questions/Comments:

Parent Signature: _____

Lesson Date: _____

Lesson Recap

In today's lesson, we worked on:

What went well:

What was challenging:

My main goal for the next week is:

Teacher comments:

Practice Plan

This week, I will practice _____ minutes per day for _____ days.

What to Practice:	What to Focus On:	Su M Tu W Th F Sa
		♩♩♩♩♩♩♩
		♩♩♩♩♩♩♩
		♩♩♩♩♩♩♩
		♩♩♩♩♩♩♩
		♩♩♩♩♩♩♩
		♩♩♩♩♩♩♩
		♩♩♩♩♩♩♩
		♩♩♩♩♩♩♩

Practice Time (min)	Su	M	Tu	W	Th	F	Sa	Total

Weekly Recap

What went well this week:

What was challenging this week:

Questions/Comments:

Parent Signature: _____

Lesson Date: _____

Lesson Recap

In today's lesson, we worked on:

What went well:

What was challenging:

My main goal for the next week is:

Teacher comments:

Practice Plan

This week, I will practice _____ minutes per day for _____ days.

What to Practice:	What to Focus On:	Su M Tu W Th F Sa
		♩ ♩ ♩ ♩ ♩ ♩ ♩
		♩ ♩ ♩ ♩ ♩ ♩ ♩
		♩ ♩ ♩ ♩ ♩ ♩ ♩
		♩ ♩ ♩ ♩ ♩ ♩ ♩
		♩ ♩ ♩ ♩ ♩ ♩ ♩
		♩ ♩ ♩ ♩ ♩ ♩ ♩
		♩ ♩ ♩ ♩ ♩ ♩ ♩
		♩ ♩ ♩ ♩ ♩ ♩ ♩

Practice Time (min)	Su	M	Tu	W	Th	F	Sa	Total

Weekly Recap

What went well this week:

What was challenging this week:

Questions/Comments:

Parent Signature: _____

Lesson Date: _____

Lesson Recap

In today's lesson, we worked on:

What went well:

What was challenging:

My main goal for the next week is:

Teacher comments:

Practice Plan

This week, I will practice _____ minutes per day for _____ days.

What to Practice:	What to Focus On:	Su M Tu W Th F Sa
		♩ ♩ ♩ ♩ ♩ ♩ ♩
		♩ ♩ ♩ ♩ ♩ ♩ ♩
		♩ ♩ ♩ ♩ ♩ ♩ ♩
		♩ ♩ ♩ ♩ ♩ ♩ ♩
		♩ ♩ ♩ ♩ ♩ ♩ ♩
		♩ ♩ ♩ ♩ ♩ ♩ ♩
		♩ ♩ ♩ ♩ ♩ ♩ ♩
		♩ ♩ ♩ ♩ ♩ ♩ ♩

Practice Time (min)	Su	M	Tu	W	Th	F	Sa	Total

Weekly Recap

What went well this week:

What was challenging this week:

Questions/Comments:

Parent Signature: _____

Monthly Check–In

In the past month, I am proud that I…

In the past month, my biggest challenge was…

Just for Fun

You've worked hard this month! Take a break!

Directions: Use the clues to fill out the crossword with musical terms. (Answer key on p. 179)

Down

1. 𝅗𝅥 (two words)

3. ♪ (two words)

5. playing by plucking the strings

6. loud

7. 𝄞 (two words)

9. the speed of the music

11. raises a pitch by a half step

Across

2. ♩ (two words)

4. soft

6. lowers a pitch by a half step

8. 𝅝 (two words)

10. gradually getting louder

The Month Ahead

In the next month, I want to continue...

In the next month, I want to get better at...

In the next month, I want to learn...

Other notes:

Lesson Date: _____

Lesson Recap

In today's lesson, we worked on:

What went well:

What was challenging:

My main goal for the next week is:

Teacher comments:

Practice Plan

This week, I will practice _____ minutes per day for _____ days.

What to Practice:	What to Focus On:	Su M Tu W Th F Sa
		♩ ♩ ♩ ♩ ♩ ♩ ♩
		♩ ♩ ♩ ♩ ♩ ♩ ♩
		♩ ♩ ♩ ♩ ♩ ♩ ♩
		♩ ♩ ♩ ♩ ♩ ♩ ♩
		♩ ♩ ♩ ♩ ♩ ♩ ♩
		♩ ♩ ♩ ♩ ♩ ♩ ♩
		♩ ♩ ♩ ♩ ♩ ♩ ♩
		♩ ♩ ♩ ♩ ♩ ♩ ♩

Practice Time (min)	Su	M	Tu	W	Th	F	Sa	Total

Weekly Recap

What went well this week:

What was challenging this week:

Questions/Comments:

Parent Signature: _____

Lesson Date: _____

Lesson Recap

In today's lesson, we worked on:

What went well:

What was challenging:

My main goal for the next week is:

Teacher comments:

Practice Plan

This week, I will practice _____ minutes per day for _____ days.

What to Practice:	What to Focus On:	Su M Tu W Th F Sa
		♩ ♩ ♩ ♩ ♩ ♩ ♩
		♩ ♩ ♩ ♩ ♩ ♩ ♩
		♩ ♩ ♩ ♩ ♩ ♩ ♩
		♩ ♩ ♩ ♩ ♩ ♩ ♩
		♩ ♩ ♩ ♩ ♩ ♩ ♩
		♩ ♩ ♩ ♩ ♩ ♩ ♩
		♩ ♩ ♩ ♩ ♩ ♩ ♩
		♩ ♩ ♩ ♩ ♩ ♩ ♩

Practice Time (min)	Su	M	Tu	W	Th	F	Sa	Total

Weekly Recap

What went well this week:

What was challenging this week:

Questions/Comments:

Parent Signature: _____

Lesson Date: _____

Lesson Recap

In today's lesson, we worked on:

What went well:

What was challenging:

My main goal for the next week is:

Teacher comments:

Practice Plan

This week, I will practice _____ minutes per day for _____ days.

What to Practice:	What to Focus On:	Su	M	Tu	W	Th	F	Sa
		♩	♩	♩	♩	♩	♩	♩
		♩	♩	♩	♩	♩	♩	♩
		♩	♩	♩	♩	♩	♩	♩
		♩	♩	♩	♩	♩	♩	♩
		♩	♩	♩	♩	♩	♩	♩
		♩	♩	♩	♩	♩	♩	♩
		♩	♩	♩	♩	♩	♩	♩
		♩	♩	♩	♩	♩	♩	♩

Practice Time (min)	Su	M	Tu	W	Th	F	Sa	Total

Weekly Recap

What went well this week:

What was challenging this week:

Questions/Comments:

Parent Signature: _____

Lesson Date: _____

Lesson Recap

In today's lesson, we worked on:

What went well:

What was challenging:

My main goal for the next week is:

Teacher comments:

Practice Plan

This week, I will practice _____ minutes per day for _____ days.

What to Practice:	What to Focus On:	Su	M	Tu	W	Th	F	Sa
		♩	♩	♩	♩	♩	♩	♩
		♩	♩	♩	♩	♩	♩	♩
		♩	♩	♩	♩	♩	♩	♩
		♩	♩	♩	♩	♩	♩	♩
		♩	♩	♩	♩	♩	♩	♩
		♩	♩	♩	♩	♩	♩	♩
		♩	♩	♩	♩	♩	♩	♩
		♩	♩	♩	♩	♩	♩	♩

Practice Time (min)	Su	M	Tu	W	Th	F	Sa	Total

Weekly Recap

What went well this week:

What was challenging this week:

Questions/Comments:

Parent Signature: _____

Monthly Check-In

In the past month, I am proud that I...

In the past month, my biggest challenge was...

You made it through a whole year of practice!

Great job!

The Year in Review

In the past year, I am proud that I...	My biggest challenge this year was...
My favorite song I learned this year was...	The hardest song I learned this year was...

The Year in Review

Next year, I want to get better at...

Next year, I want to learn...

Next year, I want to continue...

Other notes:

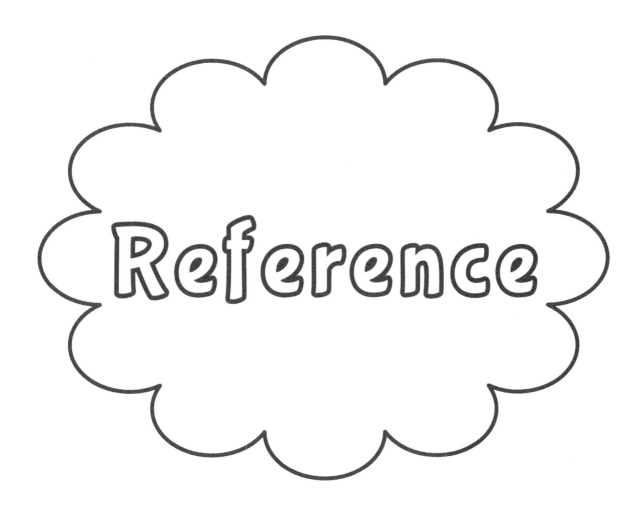

Cello Fingering Chart

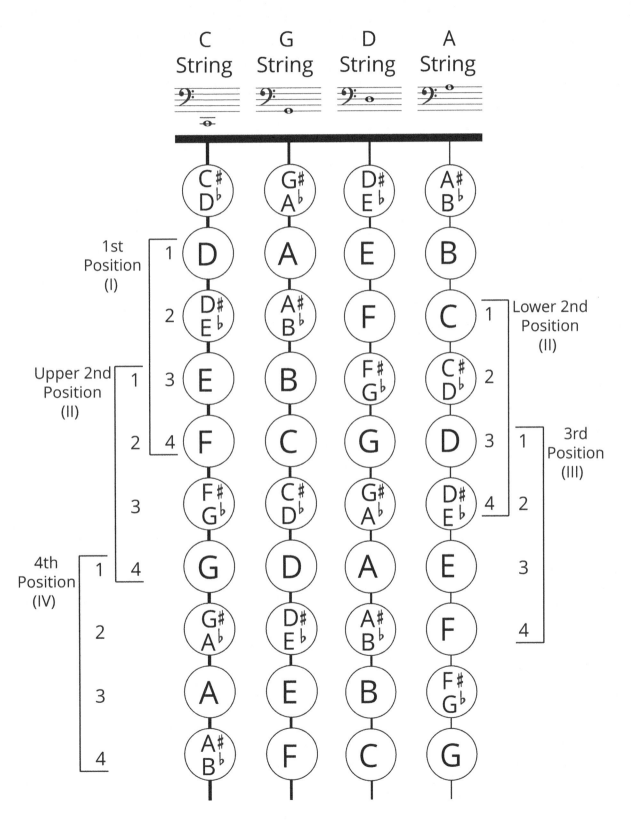

Glossary of Musical Terms

A tempo	returning to the original speed
Accelerando	gradually getting faster
Accent (>)	sign indicating that a note should be stressed
Adagio	slowly
Allegretto	moderately fast
Allegro	quickly, happily
Andante	walking pace
Arco	bow; usually used to indicate a return to bowing after a section of pizzicato
Arpeggio	a chord with the notes played in succession
Bow lift (ʼ)	sign indicating that the player should lift the bow and return it to its starting point
Chord	three or more notes played at the same time
Coda (⊕)	an added ending to a piece
Common time (C)	another way of indicating $\frac{4}{4}$ time
Crescendo ($<$)	gradually getting louder
Cut time (¢)	another way of indicating $\frac{2}{2}$ time
Da Capo (D.C.) al Fine	repeat the piece from the beginning until the word "fine"
Dal Segno (D.S.) al Fine	repeat the piece from the 𝄋 sign until the word "fine"
Dal Segno (D.S.) al Coda	repeat the piece from the 𝄋 sign and then proceed to the coda (⊕) where indicated
Decrescendo ($>$)	gradually getting softer
Diminuendo	gradually getting softer
Down bow (⊓)	a stroke of the bow in the direction from frog to tip
Dynamics	the levels of loudness and intensity in the music
Fermata (𝄐)	hold the note under the sign longer than usual
Flat (♭)	lowers a pitch by one half step
Forte (f)	loud

Fortissimo ($f\!f$)	very loud
Harmonics	overtones of the string produced when the string is lightly touched at certain points
Interval	the distance between two notes
Largo	very slowly
Legato	connected smoothly
Mezzo forte (mf)	medium-loud
Mezzo piano (mp)	medium-soft
Moderato	moderate pace
Pianissimo (pp)	very soft
Piano (p)	soft
Pitch	how high or low a note is
Pizzicato	played by plucking the strings rather than with the bow
Prestissimo	very fast
Presto	fast
Ritardando	gradually getting slower
Sharp (♯)	raises a pitch by one half step
Sforzando (sfz)	suddenly loud on one note or chord
Slur	a curve over two or more notes of different tones; indicates that the notes should be played legato
Staccato (·)	short, detached tones played while the bow remains on the string
Tempo	speed
Tie	curve connecting two notes of the same tone; indicates that the first note should be played and held for the duration of both notes
Up bow (∨)	a stroke of the bow in the direction from tip to frog
Vibrato	slight repeated change in pitch used for expression, created by rocking the fingertip on the left hand

Answer Key

p. 35

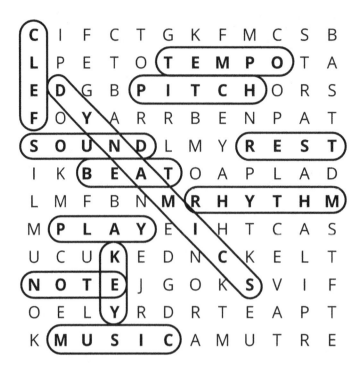

p. 47

Answer Key

p. 59

p. 71

Answer Key

p. 83

1. CELLO
2. PRACTICE
3. NOTES
4. RHYTHM
5. REST
6. BOWING
7. SCALES
8. SHARP
9. TEMPO
10. DYNAMICS

p. 107

Answer Key

p. 131

1. BEETHOVEN
2. MOZART
3. WAGNER
4. TCHAIKOVSKY

p. 155

179

Notes

Notes

Notes

Notes

Notes

Notes